Contents

CHAPTER 1

WHAT IS PASSIVE INCOME

Passive profits include ordinary profits from a source aside from an organization or contractor. The Internal Revenue Service (IRS) says passive income can come from sources: rental assets or a business in which one does now not actively take part, inclusive of being paid book royalties or stock dividends. While legally that's genuine, in exercise passive earnings may additionally take other kinds.

"Many people suppose that a passive earnings is set getting something for nothing," says financial train and retired hedge fund supervisor Todd Tresidder. "It has a 'get-rich-quick' enchantment... however ultimately, it still entails effort. You just give the work upfront."

In practice, you can do a little or all the effort prematurely, however passive earnings frequently entails a few extra labor along the way, too. Maybe you ought to keep your product up to date or your condo assets nicely-maintained which will keep the passive dollars flowing.

But in case you're dedicated to the approach, it can be a first rate way to generate income and also you'll create a few greater economic security for yourself along the way.

It's smooth to discover a certified economic guide to guide you through life style's maximum important economic decisions.

NOTE: Passive earnings is not

* Your task. Generally, passive earnings isn't always income that comes from something you've been materially concerned in consisting of the wages you earn from a task.

* A 2nd process. Getting a 2d activity isn't going to qualify as a passive profits stream because you'll nonetheless want to reveal up and do the work to get paid. A passive profit is ready creating a regular move of profits without you having to do a variety of effort to get it.

* Non-profits-generating property. Investing can be a tremendous manner to generate passive income, but handiest if the belongings

you own pay dividends or interest. Non-dividend-paying stocks or belongings like crypto currencies may be interesting, but they gained earn you passive profits.

25 passive earnings ideas for constructing wealth

If you're thinking about growing a passive earnings circulate, check out these strategies and analyze what it takes to be successful with them, whilst also expertise the risks associated with every idea.

1. DEVELOP A PATH

One famous method for passive income is creating an audio or video path, then kicking lower back at the same time as coins rolls in from the sale of your product. Courses may be allotted and bought via websites along with Udemy, Skill Share and Coursera. Alternatively, you would possibly take into account a "freemium version" constructing up a following with free content material and then charging for greater detailed data or for those who need to realize more. For example, language teachers and inventory-choosing recommendation may use this model. The free content material acts as a demonstration of your know-how and might appeal to those trying to go to the next degree.

Opportunity: A route can supply an wonderful income stream, due to the fact you're making money without difficulty after the preliminary outlay of time.

Risk: "It takes a massive amount of attempt to create the product," Tresidder says. "And to make good money from it, it has to be tremendous. There's no room for trash available."

Tresidder says you need to construct a robust platform, marketplace your merchandise and plan for extra merchandise if you need to achieve success.

"One product is not a business except you get truly lucky," Tresidder says. "The best manner to sell a current product is to create more fantastic merchandise."

Once you grasp the business version, you may generate a very good profits stream, he says.

2. WRITING AN E-BOOK AND PUBLISHING

Writing an e-book may be a great opportunity to take gain of the low value of publishing or even leverage the global distribution of Amazon to get your e book visible by doubtlessly millions of would-be shoppers. E-books may be particularly brief, possibly 30-50 pages, and can be pretty reasonably-priced to create, since they rely upon your own understanding.

You'll need to be an professional on a selected topic, however the topic might be niche and use some special abilities or skills that only a few provide but that many readers want. You can speedy design the e-book on a web platform and then even check-marketplace unique titles and charge factors.

But similar to with designing a path, a variety of the price comes when you upload extra e-books to the mix, drawing in more clients for your content material.

Opportunity: An e-book can feature no longer handiest to supply accurate records and fee to readers, but also as a way to pressure visitors for your other services, along with audio or video publications, other e-books, a internet site or probably higher-value seminars.

Risk: Your e-book has to be very sturdy to accumulate a following after which it allows if you have some way to market it, too, together with an present internet site, a merchandising on different relevant web sites, appearances within the media or podcasts or something else. So you may put in plenty of effort upfront and get little or no again on your efforts, especially at first.

And at the same time as an e-book is great, it'll help in case you write more after which even build a enterprise around the book or make the e book just one part of your commercial enterprise that strengthens the other components. So your largest risk might be that you waste your time with little praise.

3. RENTAL EARNINGS

Investing in apartment properties is an effective manner to earn passive earnings. But it often requires extra effort than people expect.

If you don't take the time to learn how to make it a profitable challenge, you may lose your funding after which a few, says John H. Graves, an Accredited Investment Fiduciary (AIF) in the Los Angeles area and writer of "The 7% Solution: You Can Afford a Comfortable Retirement." Opportunity: To earn passive profits from condominium residences, Graves says you should determine three matters:

* How tons go back you want on the funding
* The asset's total expenses and charges
* The monetary risks of proudly owning the assets

For instance, in case your aim is to earn $10,000 a year in condo cash float and the property has a month-to-month mortgage of $2,000 and expenses every other $300 a month for taxes and different costs, you'd should charge $3,133 in monthly hire to attain your purpose.

Risk: There are a few inquiries to recall: Is there a marketplace for your house? What in case you get a tenant who can pay late or damages the assets? What if you're unable to lease out your home? Any of those elements ought to place a huge dent to your passive income.

And monetary downturns can pose challenges, too. You might also all at once have tenants who can not pay their lease, even as you could nevertheless have a mortgage of your own to pay. Or you may now not be capable of lease the home out for as a whole lot as you can before, as incomes decline. And home expenses rose quick due in component to pretty low loan rates, so your rents won't be able to cover your expenses. You'll want to weigh those risks and feature contingency plans in region to shield yourself.

4. ADVERTISING AFFILIATE PROGRAM

With associate advertising, internet site proprietors, social media "influencers" or bloggers promote a third birthday celebration's product through including a link to the product on their website online or social media account. Amazon might be the exceptional acknowledged associate partner, however eBay, Awin and ShareASale are among the larger names, too. And Instagram and TikTok have turn out to be big structures for the ones trying to grow a following and sell products.

You can also don't forget growing an electronic mail listing to attract interest for your blog or in any other case direct humans to products and services that they may want.

Opportunity: When a vacationer clicks at the hyperlink and makes a buy from the 1/3-party affiliate, the site proprietor earns a fee. The commission may range from three to 7 percent, so it will in all likelihood take enormous traffic for your website to generate critical profits. But if you could grow your following or have a more profitable niche (which include software, financial offerings or fitness), you may be capable of make a few extreme coin.

Affiliate advertising is considered passive due to the fact, in theory, you may earn money simply with the aid of adding a hyperlink in your web site or social media account. In fact, you received earn something if you could't appeal to readers for your site to click at the hyperlink and buy something.

Risk: If you're just starting out, you'll need to take time to create content material and build site visitors. It can take full-size time to build a following, and also you'll ought to discover the proper components for attracting that target market, a manner that itself would possibly take some time. Worse, after you've spent all that energy, your target audience can be apt to escape to the following famous influencer, trend or social media platform.

5. FLIP RETAIL MERCHANDISE

Take gain of on-line sales structures together with eBay or Amazon, and sell products which you find at cut-price prices somewhere else. You'll arbitrage the distinction for your purchase and sale charges, and may be capable of construct a following of folks who tune your deals.

Opportunity: You'll be able to take gain of charge differences among what you can find and what the average purchaser can be able to find. This could effort especially properly if you have a touch who allows you to get entry to discounted products that few other people can find. Or you will be capable of locate precious products that others have in reality ignored. Risk: While income can happen at any time online, assisting make this approach passive, you'll without a doubt should hustle to discover a dependable source of products. Plus, you'll ought to invest money in all your products until they do sell, so you need a robust supply of cash. You'll have to actually know the market so that you're no longer buying at a rate that's too excessive. Otherwise, you could come to be with merchandise that no person wishes or whose charge you need to notably reduce as a way to promote.

6. ADVERTISING AND SELLING OF PHOTOGRAPHY ON-LINE

Selling pictures on line won't be the most apparent location to installation a passive commercial enterprise, but it may assist you to scale your efforts, specifically if you may promote the same snap shots time and again again. To do this, you might work with an enterprise which includes Getty Images, Shutter stock or Alamy.

To get started out, you'll have to be accredited with the aid of the platform, and then you license your photos to be used by whoever downloads them. The platform then will pay you whenever a person makes use of your photo. You'll need pictures that enchantment to a specific audience or that constitute a positive scene, and also you'll need to tease out in which the call for is. Photos might be pictures with fashions, landscapes, innovative eventualities and extra, or they could capture real events that could make the information.

Opportunity: Part of the fee of promoting or licensing your pix via a platform is that you have the potential to scale your efforts, specifically if you may provide photos a good way to be in demand. That means you may doubtlessly promote the identical photograph loads or hundreds of times or greater.

Risk: You ought to upload hundreds of pics to a platform including Getty Images and now not have any of them virtually generate significant income. Only a few photographs may additionally power all of your sales, so you need to maintain including pictures as you search for that needle in the haystack.

It may additionally require massive effort to go out and shoot pix, then process them and maintain up with the occasions that could in the long run drive your revenue. And motivation may be difficult to hold: Every next photograph is probably your lottery ticket, though it almost really received.

7. BUY CROWD FUNDED ACTUAL ESTATE

If you're inquisitive about investing in real estate but don't need to do a variety of the heavy lifting (control, repairs, managing tenants and extra), then any other alternative is using a crowd funding platform to invest in belongings. An skilled making an investment group selections out the real estate, after which you may determine to spend money on it and how much you're cushty with.

You'll pay an annual control price to the real property platform and have minimum funding quantities that would range from ten dollars to tens of lots of greenbacks.

Opportunity: You can get get right of entry to to private real property offers that may be attractive, and they've been preselected by way of knowledgeable buyers. You can test out the returns on the structures, so you'll have some idea of what level of returns you could count on and over what time frame. Real property investments also can assist diversify your portfolio, supporting to smooth your returns. Some systems put money into fairness (stock), while others spend money on debt. Generally, inventory gives high returns in exchange for greater chance, even as debt gives decrease returns in change for much less hazard. Some structures require you to be an accredited investor, with a sure minimal earnings or property. Popular platforms encompass Fund rise, Yield street and Diversy Fund.

Risk: You're at the hook to make your personal investments on many crowd funding structures. So at the same time as beyond returns may look proper, they're no predictor of destiny achievement. And you must make the judgment name about what to shop for. That approach you'll need to examine the prospectus for every deal you're interested by and apprehend the pros and cons.

In addition, actual estate is normally funded with high levels of debt financing, making it more susceptible to any monetary downturn. You'll also need to understand how long your cash might be locked up within the investment and whilst you may get right of entry to it, especially in an emergency.

8. PEER-TO-PEER LENDING

A peer-to-peer (P2P) mortgage is a non-public loan made among you and a borrower, facilitated thru a third-birthday celebration middleman such as Prosper. Other gamers encompass Lending Club and Upstart.

Opportunity: As a lender, you earn earnings via interest bills made on the loans. But due to the fact the mortgage is unsecured, you could become with not anything inside the event of a default.

To cut that chance, you need to do matters:

* Diversify your lending portfolio with the aid of making investment smaller amounts over more than one loans. At Prosper.Com, the minimum funding in line with mortgage is $25.

* Analyze historical data on the prospective borrowers to make informed picks.

Risk: It takes time to grasp the metrics of P2P lending, so it's no longer absolutely passive, and you'll need to cautiously vet your prospective borrowers. Since you're investing in a couple of loans, you need to pay close interest to payments received. Whatever you're making in hobby must be reinvested in case you want to construct earnings.

Economic recessions also can make high-yielding non-public loans a much more likely candidate for default, too, so those loans may go awful at higher than historical charges when the financial system worsens.

9. SHARES

Shareholders in corporations with dividend-yielding stocks receive a charge at ordinary periods from the business enterprise.

Companies pay coins dividends on a quarterly foundation out of their earnings, and all you want to do is own the inventory. Dividends are paid consistent with proportion of inventory, so the extra stocks you very own, the higher your payout.

Opportunity: Since the profits from the stocks isn't related to any activity other than the initial economic investment, owning dividend-yielding shares may be one of the most passive types of making a living. The cash will absolutely be deposited in your brokerage account.

Risk: The complicated part is choosing the proper shares.

For example, businesses issuing a completely high dividend might not be able to maintain it. Graves warns that too many beginners leap into the marketplace without thoroughly investigating the business enterprise issuing the stock. "You've got to analyze every agency's website and be cushy with their economic statements," Graves says. "You need to spend to a few weeks investigating each business enterprise."

That said, there are ways to spend money on dividend-yielding stocks without spending a large quantity of time comparing businesses. Graves advises going with change-traded funds, or ETFs. ETFs are investment budget that maintain assets inclusive of stocks, commodities and bonds, but they change like stocks. ETFs also diversify your holdings, so if one employer cuts its payout, it doesn't affect the ETF's rate or dividend too much. Here are some of the exceptional ETFs to pick from. "ETFs are a perfect preference for beginners because they are smooth to apprehend, highly liquid, less expensive and feature some distance higher capacity returns due to a ways lower charges than mutual budget," Graves says. Another key threat is that shares or ETFs can flow down extensively in quick intervals of time, especially throughout times of uncertainty, as in 2020 whilst the corona virus crisis stunned economic markets. Economic pressure can also purpose a few corporations to reduce their dividends totally, whilst diversified finances can also feel much less of a pinch.

Compare your investing alternatives with Bankrate's brokerage evaluations.

10. DEVELOPING AN APP

Creating an app could be a way to make that prematurely funding of time after which achieve the reward over the lengthy haul. Your app might be a game or one which enables mobile customers carry out some tough-to-do characteristic. Once your app is public, customers download it, and you could generate income.

Opportunity: An app has large upside, if you may layout something that catches the flowery of your audience. You'll must remember how great to generate sales out of your app. For example, you may run in-app advertisements or in any other case have customers pay a nominal rate for downloading the app.

If your app profits reputation or you get hold of feedback, you'll in all likelihood need to feature incremental features to preserve the app relevant and famous.

Risk: The biggest chance here is probably that you use some time unprofitably. If you devote very little cash to the assignment (or money which you could have spent besides, for instance, on hardware), you have got little economic downside. However, it's a crowded market and clearly successful apps ought to offer a compelling price or revel in to users. You'll additionally want to ensure that if your app collects any records that it's in compliance with privacy legal guidelines, which range across the globe. The recognition of apps may be quick-lived, too, that means your coins flow may want to dry up loads quicker than you expect.

11. RENT OUT A PARKING SPACE

Do you have a parking area that you're no longer using or that could be utilized by someone else? You ought to alternate that spot for some cash. It will be an even higher set-up when you have a bigger place that could match several motors or that could be useful for multiple activities or venues.

Opportunity: In mainly excessive-call for areas or at some stage in high-call for times (as an example, at some stage in a live performance or carrying event), your parking spot will be worth real cash. For example, in case you live near a place that has common commuters but this is strapped for parking spots, you may have a cash-maker on your palms. You may have the excellent chance of turning a income via renting to a person who desires the spot on a daily foundation, in preference to for one-off events.

Risk: This concept might not be specially risky, however you do want to make certain you aren't violating any restrictions from your location of house or different entity through renting out a parking space. It's in all likelihood profitable having a disclaimer of legal responsibility as a circumstance of parking for your spot, too.

12. REITS

A REIT is a real estate funding trust, which is a fancy call for a corporation that owns and manages real property. REITs have a unique criminal shape so that they pay little or no company profits tax in the event that they pass along most in their earnings to shareholders. Opportunity: You should purchase REITs at the inventory market similar to some other company or dividend stock. You'll earn whatever the REIT can pay out as a dividend, and the high-quality REITs have a document of increasing their dividend on an annual foundation, so you may want to have a developing stream of dividends through the years.

Like dividend shares, man or woman REITs can be riskier than owning an ETF inclusive of dozens of REIT shares. A fund provides immediate diversification and is usually a lot safer than shopping for individual stocks — and also you'll nonetheless get a pleasing payout.

Risk: Just like dividend shares, you'll have on the way to choose the best REITs, and meaning you'll need to research every of the corporations which you might buy — a time-consuming procedure. And whilst it's a passive hobby, you can lose plenty of money if you don't realize what you're doing. Like any inventory, the rate can range plenty in the short term.

REIT dividends aren't covered from hard financial instances, either. If the REIT doesn't generate sufficient profits, it will likely need to reduce its dividend or take away it completely. So your passive income can also get hit simply when you need it most.

13. A BOND LADDER:

A bond ladder is a chain of bonds that mature at one-of-a-kind instances over a length of years. The staggered maturities let you decrease reinvestment danger, which is the threat of reinvesting your cash when bonds provide too-low interest bills.

Opportunity: A bond ladder is a conventional passive funding that has appealed to retirees and near-retirees for decades. You can sit down again and acquire your hobby payments, and when the bond matures, you "amplify the ladder," rolling that foremost into a new set of bonds. For instance, you would possibly start with bonds of one year, three years, 5 years and 7 years.

In a 12 months, whilst the primary bond matures, you've got bonds remaining of two years, four years and 6 years. You can use the proceeds from the currently matured bond to buy some other three hundred and sixty five days or roll out to a longer duration, for instance, an 8-year bond.

Risk: A bond ladder removes one of the main risks of purchasing bonds – the danger that after your bond matures you've got to buy a brand new bond when hobby prices won't be favorable.

Bonds come with other risks, too. While Treasury bonds are backed with the aid of the federal authorities, company bonds aren't, so you should lose your most important if the business enterprise defaults. And you'll want to very own many bonds to diversify your danger and take away the risk of any single bond hurting your average portfolio. If general interest fees upward thrust, it could push down the cost of your bonds.

Because of those concerns, many buyers flip to bond ETFs, which give a varied fund of bonds that you may installation right into a ladder, disposing of the hazard of a unmarried bond hurting your returns.

14. ADVERTISE POSTS ON SOCIAL MEDIA

Do you have a sturdy following on social media inclusive of Instagram or TikTok? Get growing client manufacturers to pay you to submit approximately their product or in any other case characteristic it in your feed.

You'll want to hold filling your profile with content that attracts on your target audience, even though. And meaning continuing to create posts that develop your attain and interact your fans on social media.

Opportunity: Leveraging your social media presence is an appealing enterprise version. Draw eyeballs and clicks for your profile with strong content material and then monetize that content through setting up backed posts from brands that appeal in your followers.

Risk: Getting started here can be a Catch-22: You want a large audience to get meaningful subsidized posts, but you're not an attractive choice till you get a significant target audience. So you'll need to awareness a variety of time first on developing your target audience and not using a assure which you'll achieve success. You can come to be spending heaps of time following the tendencies and building content material, within the hopes that you in the end get the sponsorship which you're aiming for. Even when you've were given the sponsored posts you're looking for, you'll need to maintain posting to attract on your target audience and continue to be an attractive choice for advertisers. That way committing to extra time and financial investment, even in case you do have plenty of autonomy on exactly while to do it.

15. INVEST IN A HIGH-YIELD CD OR FINANCIAL SAVINGS ACCOUNT

Investing in a excessive-yield certificate of deposit (CD) or financial savings account at a web bank can will let you generate a passive earnings and additionally get one of the maximum hobby quotes within the u . S . A .. You received even need to go away your house to make money.

Opportunity: To make the maximum of your CD, you'll want to do a short search of the state's pinnacle CD charges or the top savings money owed. It's normally tons greater wonderful to go together with an internet bank as opposed to your neighborhood financial institution, due to the fact you'll be capable of choose the top charge to be had within the country. And you'll still experience a guaranteed go back of main up to $250,000, in case your financial organization is subsidized by using the FDIC.

Risk: As long as your financial institution is backed by way of the FDIC and inside limits, your most important is safe. So, making an investment in a CD or financial savings account is about as safe a return as you may locate. But that go back can fade in contrast to inflation, hurting the real purchasing power of your money. Nevertheless, a CD or financial savings account will yield higher than protecting your money in coins or in a non-hobby-bearing checking account where you'll receive not anything.

16. RENT OUT YOUR PRIVATE HOME SHORT-TERM

This truthful strategy takes advantage of space which you're no longer the use of anyway and turns it into a cash-making possibility. If you're going away for the summer or need to be out of metropolis for a while, or maybe even simply want to travel, bear in mind renting out your modern-day area even as you're long gone. Opportunity: You can listing your space on any variety of websites, inclusive of Airbnb or Vrbo, and set the condo terms yourself. You'll gather a take a look at for your efforts with minimal greater work, specially in case you're renting to a tenant who can be in region for a few months. Risk: You don't have a number of economic drawback right here, even though letting strangers live in your home is a chance that's extraordinary of maximum passive investments. Tenants might also deface or maybe destroy your private home or maybe scouse borrows valuables, for example.

17. ADVERTISE TO YOUR VEHICLE

You can be capable of earn a few extra cash through in reality using your vehicle around metropolis. Contact a specialized advertising business enterprise, with the intention to examine your driving conduct, inclusive of in which you power and how many miles. If you're a in shape with one among their advertisers, the organization will "wrap" your car with the advertisements for free of charge to you. Agencies are searching out more recent automobiles, and drivers must have a smooth using record.

Opportunity: While you do should get out and power, if you're already installing the mileage anyway, then that is a terrific manner to earn hundreds per month with very little more value. Drivers may be paid by using the mile.

Risk: If this idea looks exciting, be extra careful to find a valid operation to companion with.

Many fraudsters set up scams in this space to try to bilk you out of hundreds.

18. CREATE A WEBLOG OR YOUTUBE CHANNEL

Are you an expert on tour to Thailand? A maven of Mine craft? A sultan of swing dancing? Take your passion for a topic and turn it right into a weblog or a YouTube channel, the use of ads or sponsors to generate your earnings. Find a famous difficulty, even a small area of interest, and become a professional on it. At first, you'll need to construct out a collection of content material and draw an target audience, but it may create a regular profits circulate through the years, as you turn out to be recognized in your enticing content material.
Opportunity: You can leverage a free (or very low-value) platform, and then use your awesome content to construct a following. The more unique your voice or vicinity of hobby, the better which will grow to be "the" man or woman to follow. Then draw sponsors to you.

Risk: You'll must build out content material on the start and then create ongoing content material that can take time. And you'll want to be definitely obsessed on the product, considering the fact that that let you hold the motivation to preserve, mainly on the begin as your fans are still locating you.

The actual disadvantage right here is that you may outlay a bunch of your time and sources, with little to expose for it, if there's confined hobby in your challenge or area of interest. Your place of know-how can be too niche to honestly draw a profitable audience, but you received make certain of that until you test.

19. RENT OUT USEFUL HOUSEHOLD ITEMS

Here's a version on renting out an idle car: Start even smaller with other household objects that human beings may also need however that can be amassing dust for your garage. Lawnmowers? Power equipment? Mechanics equipment and device box? Tents or large coolers? Look for excessive-fee objects that humans need for a quick time period and in which it may not make experience for someone to own the object. Then prepare a manner for clients to find out your stock and a manner for them to pay for it. Opportunity: You can begin small right here, and then scale up if there's hobby in a specific place. Do human beings abruptly want a tent for weekend camping while the climate gets hotter or cooler? Figure out in which the demand is, and then you could even pass purchase the item, in preference to having it proper on hand. In some instances you might be capable of recoup the fee of the item after some makes use of. Risk: There's usually the opportunity that your private home is broken or stolen, however you could mitigate this threat with contracts that will let you replace the item at the customer's cost. If you start small right here, you're now not exposed to a good deal hazard, especially in case you already have the object and you're not probable to want it in the close to destiny. Pay precise attention to legal responsibility troubles, mainly if you're renting out device that has the capacity to be dangerous (e.g., power gear.)

20. SELL DESIGNS ON-LINE

If you have design competencies, you'll be in a position to turn them right into a cash maker via promoting items along with your printed designs on them. Businesses which include Café Press and Zazzle assist you to sell objects such as T-shirts, hats, mugs and extra along with your very own designs.

Opportunity: You can start with your own designs and see what the market is inquisitive about, and amplify from there. You may be able to capitalize on the surging interest in a cutting-edge event and design a blouse that captures the spirit of the times or at the least a snarky tackle it. And you could also set up your very own net storefront thru a domain consisting of Shopify to market your chocolates.

Risk: Printing companions will let you ship objects without at once making an investment within the merchandise yourself, warding off considered one of the biggest dangers of tying up your capital. But you may be able to get higher pricing if you invest in a number of the stock yourself. Another big hazard right here is that you can invest lots of time with little payoff, but this road is probably thrilling if you're already doing the layout effort for some other purpose, including private hobby.

21. SET UP AN ANNUITY

An annuity may be a terrific area to installation reliable earnings. With a standard annuity, you deliver cash to a monetary organization, usually an insurance business enterprise, so that it will provide you with a movement of income inside the destiny. Annuities pay out month-to-month, and that they can be installation in a variety of ways, as an instance to start paying at once or plenty later.

Opportunity: Annuities may be structured in a huge quantity of ways, depending on exactly what you want, however they're the definition of passive income. If you want a month-to-month payout right now, the insurance business enterprise can set that up, or you could shape the charge to start whilst you retire, for instance. In addition, you can set up an annuity that has a hard and fast go back or one that could offer a variable payout depending on how the annuity's investments executed.

An annuity can be installation to pay out for a set period, say, 20 years, or a life-time. It could give up charge on your death or it could continue paying out on your spouse. The options are huge.

Risk: Annuities are particularly complex, and while you set one up, you're often locked in for a long time, though you may be able to get out by means of paying a full-size penalty. Read the best print at the settlement carefully so you understand the professionals and cons of the particular agreement.

Every annuity settlement is different, and each may offer a completely unique set of benefits as a way to cater on your precise needs. So it's vital to understand what you're signing up for.

22. BUY A NEIGHBORHOOD BUSINESS

A nearby enterprise offers you the potential to generate a coins flow move thru an present and set up employer. If the business is profitable sufficient, you could even be capable of lease a supervisor to run it for you while you are making best the largest decisions or none at all. You can be able to get an appealing mortgage to buy it, so that you positioned less of your personal money at threat early on.

Opportunity: Local businesses may additionally have appealing and profitable niches that you may buy into, and ones that cannot be without difficulty replicated by competitors. You may be able to piggyback off the vendor's know-how or credentials, in particular on the start as you arise to hurry. Sellers can be inclined to finance part of the sale, giving them a few incentive to see the business prevail. Also, you could make part of the acquisition charge contingent on positive profit goals or different metrics.

Risk: You'll need to carefully vet any capacity acquisition applicants, lest you emerge as with a enterprise that's a great deal less worthwhile than it seems or that has fading possibilities. It can prove precious to work with skilled and honest brokers to get the satisfactory deal and avoid pitfalls, or lease a consultant to help evaluate a potential deal. In addition, in case you're hiring a supervisor to run the store, you'll want to be sure they're sincere and competent, otherwise you'll have troubles.

23. BUY A WEBLOG

If you need to get into the running a blog recreation, do not forget shopping for one and skipping the line on constructing it. You can get the contacts and relationships of the previous proprietor and may be able to bring your personal, too. And you could be producing income from day one in place of building and hoping.

Opportunity: Buying a blog gets you in the sport today as opposed to the next day, however you'll want to be already informed and captivated with the issue. It could be even better if you have a few thoughts to enhance the blog (higher content, higher performance, decrease expenses, and so on.) so you can leverage it into extra profitability than might have been indicated with the aid of the acquisition rate.

Risk: A blog, like every commercial enterprise, is not that liquid, so if you decide you want to move on to something greener, you can not get what you paid for it or maybe be able to sell it at all. And of path, you have got with a view to gauge the market correctly, generating content material that readers want or that draws sponsors or other sales drivers.

24. BUY PREFERRED INVENTORY

Preferred inventory is a type of stock that acts greater like a bond, making attractively large dividend payouts on a quarterly agenda. Like bonds, preferred inventory has a face value and can have a specific maturity, even though it is able to additionally be perpetual, that means the organisation want by no means redeem it. Typically, it may be redeemed after 5 years of issuance. Preferred stocks alternate on an exchange, so that you can purchase them without problems, and liquidity is pretty exact. Opportunity: Preferred stock can pay out large-than-usual dividends, compared to a corporation's bonds, but that's in exchange for forgoing a capital benefit (unless you purchase preferred at a reduction to their face fee). But it is able to be an attractive manner to earn a passive go back. Many REITs, banks and different economic businesses issue preferred to finance their operations.

Risk: Preferred shares trade on an alternate, which means that their prices will range, especially in response to adjustments in prevailing interest costs. As quotes upward thrust, the rate of preferred will probably fall, and vice versa, though the price possibly gained upward push much above face price. And like bonds, you'll want to cautiously recognize the organization and its ability to pay its dividends, or your funding may want to completely decline price.

If you don't want to pick out man or woman preferred shares, then choose a desired inventory fund. You'll get a various series of preferred, decreasing your danger.

25. INVEST IN A MUNICIPAL BOND CLOSED-GIVE UP FUND

Municipal bonds offer tax-unfastened dividend profits to buyers in trade for financing public initiatives for states and towns. A closed-end fund centered in this place of the market owns a number of these bonds after which juices the overall return by borrowing money to shop for extra. Like investing in CDs or dividend funds, a closed-give up fund is the maximum passive type of profits.

Opportunity: A closed-cease municipal bond fund can be an appealing manner to earn tax-unfastened earnings, which may be particularly for those in excessive-tax states or excessive tax brackets. These funds typically pay better dividends than a median municipal bond because they use leverage (itself a threat), although a fund owns a number of extraordinary bonds, helping to lessen average risk. Closed-end price range must typically be purchased at a great bargain to their internet asset value, assisting reduce threat, too.

Risk: Bond charges and consequently the price of bond funds decline whilst hobby prices rise (and vice versa). But a closed-stop fund's leverage magnifies this effect, so the common fund will decline greater than the average bond in a downturn. At the same time, the bond fund may additionally need to reduce its payout with the intention to pay improved expenses on its borrowing, hitting the fund's fee nonetheless extra. So a closed-end fund may be risky as quotes shift quickly.

Which passive earnings supply is great?

The query of which passive profits supply is best relies upon on numerous factors, however some of the most essential include the quantity of cash you have to make investments, the entire opportunity size, your hobby and capability in the place, the quantity of time you need to make investments and the capacity to prevail. Typically, the decrease the obstacles to access, the extra crowded the sphere of competition and the decrease probability of fulfillment. So you'll want to weigh the opportunity in opposition to those elements and notice which passive income strategy works high-quality for you. But it is able to be useful to have herbal capacity and an hobby on your target vicinity, due to the fact those can assist inspire you inside the early days when matters are probably to be tougher.

There are passive earnings possibilities for folks who are starting out with some money and even those who've no cash to start.

How can I make passive profits without money? If you have little or no cash to start, you'll should rely totally on your very own time investment to power you thru, at least until you building up touch money. That manner that specialize in passive profits resources that take advantage of the subsequent developments:

* An place wherein you're an professional. Here you could construct your expertise right into a beneficial products or services for purchasers, e.g. Design, software program coding and others.

* An in advance effort-heavy possibility. You'll want an possibility that calls for a time or work funding, which include developing a course, constructing out an influencer profile or different alternatives.

In impact, you're substituting a while on your loss of capital, till you can get enough capital to extend your set of possibilities.

How can I make passive earnings with cash?

Money can provide you with greater passive investment possibilities. If you have cash to spend money on a passive possibility, you have not handiest the opportunity set above however a brand new range, too. Money is a prerequisite for taking gain of the subsequent passive profits areas:

* Investing in dividend shares, favored shares or REITs. Investing in stocks way you want money in advance, but you'll acquire a number of the most passive sorts of income around.

* Save with bonds or CDs. Other in simple terms passive sports include buying bonds or CDs.

Here you can use your money to make cash with very little effort in your element, if that's what you'd love to do. Of direction, you may pair your money with quite a few time investment to transport into a fair more moneymaking area of interest, too.

How many income streams must you've got? There is not any "one length suits all" advice with regards to producing profits streams. How many sources of profits you have to depend upon in which you're financially, and what your economic goals for the destiny are. But having at the least a few is a good begin.

"You'll seize extra fish with multiple strains within the water," says Greg McBride, CFA, leader monetary analyst at Bank rate. "In addition to the earned profits generated from your human capital, condominium homes, income-producing securities and business ventures are a superb way to diversify your income circulate."

Of course, you'll want to make certain that putting effort into a new passive profits movement isn't inflicting you to lose awareness for your different streams. So you do need to balance your efforts and make certain you're choosing the great possibilities for your time.

47

48